**Practical**
**Pre-School** Books

**Match your theme to the 2014 EYFS**

# Planning for Learning through
# All about me

by Rachel Sparks Linfield and Penny Coltman. Illustrated by Cathy Hughes

## Contents

Published by Practical Pre-School Books, A Division of MA Education Ltd,
St Jude's Church, Dulwich Road, Herne Hill, London, SE24 0PB   Tel. 020 7738 5454
www.pracalpreschoolbooks.com

Updated and reprinted 2015. Revised (3rd edition) 2013 © MA Education Ltd. Revised edition © MA Education Ltd 2008.
First edition © Step Forward Publishing Limited 2001.

Front and back cover images taken by Lucie Carlier © MA Education Ltd.

Planning for Learning through All about me ISBN: 978 1 909280 32 8

# Making plans

## Child-friendly planning

The purpose of planning is to make sure that all children enjoy a broad and balanced experience of learning. Planning should be flexible, useful and child-friendly. It should reflect opportunities available both indoors and outside. Plans form part of a planning cycle in which practitioners make observations, assess and plan.

Children benefit from reflective planning that takes into account the children's current interests and abilities and also allows them to take the next steps in their learning. Plans should make provision for activity that promotes learning and a desire to imagine, observe, communicate, experiment, investigate and create.

Plans should include a variety of types of activity. Some will be adult-initiated or adult-led, that focus on key skills or concepts. These should be balanced with opportunities for child-initiated activity where the children take a key role in the planning. In addition there is a need to plan for the on-going continuous provision areas such as construction, sand and water, malleable materials, small world, listening area, role-play and mark-making. Thought also needs to be given to the enhanced provision whereby an extra resource or change may enable further exploration, development and learning.

The outdoor environment provides valuable opportunities for children's learning. It is vital that plans value the use of outdoor space.

## The UK Frameworks

Within the UK a number of frameworks exist to outline the provision that children should be entitled to receive. Whilst a variety of terms and labels are used to describe the Areas of Learning there are key principles which are common to each document. For example they advocate that practitioners' planning should be personal based on observations and knowledge of the specific children within a setting. They acknowledge that young children learn best when there is scope for child-initiated activity. In addition it is accepted that young children's learning is holistic. Although within the documents Areas of Learning are presented separately to ensure that key areas are not over-looked, within settings, children's learning will combine

areas. Thus the Areas of Learning are perhaps of most use for planning, assessment and recording.

## Focused area plans

The plans you make for each day will outline areas of continuous provision and focused, adult-led activities. Plans for focused-area activities need to include aspects such as:

- Resources needed
- The way in which you might introduce activities
- Individual needs
- The organisation of adult help
- Size of the group
- Timing
- Safety
- Key vocabulary.

Identify the learning and the Early Learning Goals that each activity is intended to promote. Make a note of any assessments or observations that you are likely to carry out. After carrying out the activities, make notes on your plans to say what was particularly successful, or any changes you would make another time.

# Making plans

## A final note

Planning should be seen as flexible. Not all groups meet every day, and not all children attend every day. Any part of the plan can be used independently, stretched over a longer period or condensed to meet the needs of any group. You will almost certainly adapt the activities as children respond to them in different ways and bring their own ideas, interests and enthusiasms. The important thing is to ensure that the children are provided with a varied and enjoyable curriculum that meets their individual developing needs.

## Using the book

Read the section which outlines links to the Early Learning Goals (pages 4-6) and explains the rationale for focusing on 'All about me'.

The chart on page 7 gives an example format for weekly planning. It provides opportunity to plan for the on-going continuous provision, as well as more focused activities.

Use pages 8 to 19 to select from a wide range of themed, focused activities that recognise the importance of involving children in practical activities and giving them opportunities to follow their own interests. For each 'All about me' theme, two activities are described in detail as examples to help you in your planning and preparation. Key vocabulary, questions and learning opportunities are identified. Use the activities as a basis to:

●     Extend current and emerging interests and capabilities
●     Engage in sustained conversations
●     Stimulate new interests and skills.

Find out on page 20 how the All about me activities can be brought together in a 'Disguises Event'.

Use page 21 for ideas of resources to collect or prepare. Remember that the books listed are only suggestions. It is likely that you will already have within your setting a variety of other books that will be equally useful.

The activity overview chart on page 23 can be used either at the planning stage or after each theme has been completed. It will help you to see at a glance which aspects of children's

development are being addressed and alert you to the areas which may need greater input in the future.

As children take part in the activities, their learning will progress. 'Collecting evidence' on page 24 explains how you might monitor each child's achievements.

There is additional material to support the working partnership of families and children in the form of a reproducible Family page found inside the back cover.

It is important to appreciate that the ideas presented in this book will only be a part of your planning. Many activities that will be taking place as routine in your group may not be mentioned. For example, it is assumed that sand, dough, water, puzzles, role-play, floor toys, technology and large scale apparatus are part of the ongoing early years experience. Role-play areas, stories, rhymes, singing, and group discussion times are similarly assumed to be happening in each week although they may not be a focus for described activities.

# Using the 'Early Learning Goals'

The principles that are common to each of the United Kingdom curriculum frameworks for the early years are described on page 2. It is vital that, when planning for children within a setting, practitioners are familiar with the relevant framework's content and organisation for areas of learning. Regardless however, of whether a child attends a setting in England, Northern Ireland, Scotland or Wales they have a right to provision for all areas of learning. The children should experience activities which encourage them to develop their communication and language; personal, social, emotional, physical, mathematical and creative skills. They should have opportunities within literacy and be encouraged to understand and explore their world.

Within the Statutory Framework for the Early Years Foundation Stage (2014), Communication and Language; Physical Development and Personal, Social and Emotional Development are described as Prime Areas of Learning that are 'particularly crucial for igniting children's curiosity and enthusiasm for learning, and for building their capacity to learn, form relationships and thrive' (page 7, DfE 2014). The Specific Areas of Learning are Literacy, Mathematics, Understanding the World and Expressive Arts and Design.

For each Area of Learning the Early Learning Goals (ELGs) describe what children are expected to be able to do by the time they enter Year 1. These goals, detailed on pages 4 to 7, have been used throughout this book to show how activities relating to 'All about me' could link to these expectations. For example, for Personal, Social and Emotional Development one aim relates to the development of children's 'self-confidence and self-awareness'. Activities suggested which provide the opportunity for children to do this have the reference PSE1. This will enable you to see which parts of the Early Learning Goals are covered for a given theme and to plan for areas to be revisited and developed.

In addition, an activity may be carried out to develop a range of different Early Learning Goals. For example, whilst exploring faces children might make 'Please smile' posters and use writing skills. In addition, they will consider what makes people want to smile and use creative skills. Thus, whilst adult-focused activities may have clearly defined goals at the planning stage, it must be remembered that as children take on ideas and initiate their own learning and activities, goals may change.

## The Prime Areas of Learning
### Communication and Language

**Listening and attention:** children listen attentively in a range of situations. They listen to stories, accurately anticipating key events and respond to what they hear with relevant comments, questions or actions. They give their attention to what others say and respond appropriately, while engaged in another activity. (CL1)

**Understanding:** children follow instructions involving several ideas or actions. They answer 'how' and 'why' questions about their experiences and in response to stories or events. (CL2)

**Speaking:** children express themselves effectively, showing awareness of listeners' needs. They use past, present and future forms accurately when talking about events that have happened or are to happen in the future. They develop their own narratives and explanations by connecting ideas or events. (CL3)

'All about me' provides many opportunities for children to enjoy listening, understanding and speaking. When the children go on a sound detecting walk, or listen to a book being read, they will develop skills for CL1. Games such as 'I spy', or describing objects in a feely bag, encourage both speaking and listening as well as require the children to follow instructions. Times spent speaking about family members and events, will allow children to develop their understanding and provide occasions for children to ask and answer questions.

## Physical Development

**Moving and handling:** children show good control and co-ordination in large and small movements. They move confidently in a range of ways, safely negotiating space. They handle equipment and tools effectively, including pencils for writing. (PD1)

**Health and self-care:** children know the importance for good health of physical exercise, and a healthy diet, and talk about ways to keep healthy and safe. They manage their own basic hygiene and personal needs successfully, including dressing and going to the toilet independently. (PD2)

'All about me' offers many opportunities for children to enjoy movement activities and to handle tools and equipment. When children move and balance, or use their hands for aiming, catching and throwing to explore body parts, they can develop and demonstrate control and co-ordination. Activities relating to food, wearing appropriate clothes and taking exercise will contribute to the development of knowledge of health and self-care. Areas such as basic hygiene and going to the toilet independently, however, will be part of on-going, daily activity and, as a result, PD2 will appear less frequently than PD1 within the described activities for Physical Development.

## Personal, Social and Emotional Development

**Self-confidence and self-awareness:** children are confident to try new activities, and say why they like some activities more than others. They are confident to speak in a familiar group, will talk about their ideas, and will choose the resources they need for their chosen activities. They say when they do or don't need help. (PSE1)

**Managing feelings and behaviour:** children talk about how they and others show feelings, talk about their own and others' behaviour, and its consequences, and know that some behaviour is unacceptable. They work as part of a group or class, and understand and follow the rules. They adjust their behaviour to different situations, and take changes of routine in their stride. (PSE2)

**Making relationships:** children play co-operatively, taking turns with others. They take account of one another's ideas about how to organise their activity. They show sensitivity to others' needs and feelings, and form positive relationships with adults and other children. (PSE3)

'All about me' offers many opportunities, both for child-initiated and adult-led activities, that will develop children personally, socially and emotionally. When discussing how body parts are used, or how to handle precious objects, children have the opportunity to make relationships. When considering which clothes to wear for a variety of weather children can develop self-confidence and self-awareness. Many of the areas described within the ELGs for Personal, Social and Emotional Development though, will be covered on an almost incidental basis. Any activity that involves collaboration will help children to build relationships whilst self-confidence can be promoted through activities that allow children to show initiative and follow their own trains of thought.

# The Specific Areas of Learning
## Literacy

**Reading:** children read and understand simple sentences. They use phonic knowledge to decode regular words and read them aloud accurately. They also read some common irregular words. They demonstrate understanding when talking with others about what they have read. (L1)

**Writing:** children use their phonic knowledge to write words in ways which match their spoken sounds. They also write some irregular common words. They write simple sentences which can be read by themselves and others. Some words are spelt correctly and others are phonetically plausible. (L2)

Activities for All about me based on well-known picture books allow the children to enjoy listening to stories and to read using both their phonic knowledge and memories of common, irregular words. Discussions of the stories will help children to understand and to develop their vocabularies. Activities, such as writing menus and taking orders in the role-play healthy eating café or making 'Please smile' posters will encourage children to explore the sounds within words and to enjoy the early stages of writing.

## Mathematics

**Numbers:** children count reliably with numbers from 1 to 20, place them in order and say which number is one more or one less than a given number. Using quantities and objects, they add and subtract two single-digit numbers and count on or back to find the answer. They solve problems, including doubling, halving and sharing. (M1)

**Shape, space and measures:** children use everyday language to talk about size, weight, capacity, position, distance, time

and plants and explain why some things occur, and talk about changes. (UW2)

**Technology:** children recognise that a range of technology is used in places such as homes and schools. They select and use technology for particular purposes. (UW3)

To understand their world children need times to gain knowledge, to explore and to relate what they discover to both previously held ideas and future learning. Clearly activities relating to 'All about me' offer valuable opportunities to discover facts about bodies, the senses, health, emotions and families. When exploring hands, eyes and faces children will be able to make comparisons and notice similarities and differences between themselves and others. When on a sound detecting walk children have the opportunity to use technology. Technology will also feature in role-play as well as being part of the on-going, daily provision.

## Expressive Arts and Design

**Exploring and using media and materials:** children sing songs, make music and dance, and experiment with ways of changing them. They safely use and explore a variety of materials, tools and techniques, experimenting with colour, design, texture, form and function. (EAD1)

**Being imaginative:** children use what they have learnt about media and materials in original ways, thinking about uses and purposes. They represent their own ideas, thoughts and feelings through design and technology, art, music, dance, role-play and stories. (EAD2)

Whilst involved in activities for All about me, children will experience working with a variety of materials, tools and techniques as they paint self-portraits, make collages of faces and print with fruits and vegetables. A number of songs that have body parts have been recommended which, with the addition of actions and percussion, allow the children to be imaginative. Throughout all the activities children should be encouraged to talk about what they see and feel as they communicate their ideas in painting, collage, music and role-play.

## Note
The Early Learning Goals raise awareness of key aspects within any child's development for each Area of Learning. It is important to remember that these goals are reached through a combination of adult and child-initiated activity within Early Years settings and also a child's home life. Thus, it is vital that goals are shared by practitioners and parents, and children are given every opportunity to develop throughout their Early Years Foundation Stage at home and within a setting.

and money to compare quantities and objects and to solve problems. They recognise, create and describe patterns. They explore characteristics of everyday objects and shapes and use mathematical language to describe them. (M2)

Activities for All about me provide many opportunities for children to count, measure and explore shape and space. Observing body parts encourages children to count and to compare. Investigations of eye colour stimulates counting and grouping. The use of hand and footprints allows children to use non-standard measures and gain awareness of lengths. Role-play areas such as the healthy eating café or optician's highlight the use of numbers in everyday life.

## Understanding the World

**People and communities:** children talk about past and present events in their own lives and in the lives of family members. They know that other children don't always enjoy the same things, and are sensitive to this. They know about similarities and differences between themselves and others, and among families, communities and traditions. (UW1)

**The world:** children know about similarities and differences in relation to places, objects, materials and living things. They talk about the features of their own immediate environment and how environments might vary from one another. They make observations of animals

# Example chart to aid planning in the EYFS

| Week beginning: | Monday | Tuesday | Wednesday | Thursday | Friday |
|---|---|---|---|---|---|
| **FOCUSED ACTIVITIES** | | | | | |
| Focus Activity 1: | | | | | |
| Focus Activity 2: | | | | | |
| Stories and rhymes | | | | | |
| **CONTINUOUS PROVISION (Indoor)** | | | | | |
| Collage | | | | | |
| Construction (large) | | | | | |
| Construction (small) | | | | | |
| ICT | | | | | |
| Imaginative play | | | | | |
| Listening | | | | | |
| Malleable materials | | | | | |
| Mark making | | | | | |
| Painting | | | | | |
| Role play | | | | | |
| Sand (damp) | | | | | |
| Sand (dry) | | | | | |
| Water | | | | | |
| **CONTINUOUS PROVISION (Outdoor)** | | | | | |
| Construction | | | | | |
| Creative play | | | | | |
| Exploratory play | | | | | |
| Gross motor | | | | | |
| **ENHANCED PROVISION (Indoor)** | | | | | |
| | | | | | |
| | | | | | |
| **ENHANCED PROVISION (Outdoor)** | | | | | |
| | | | | | |
| | | | | | |

# Theme 1: My body

## Communication and Language
- During circle time show children how to roll a ball gently to a friend. On receiving the ball the child says 'my name is _____ and with my * I can _____.' Replace * with a body part ie. 'with my hands I can draw'. (CL2)
- Read *Funnybones* by Janet and Allan Ahlberg. Talk about skeletons and how they support our bodies. Re-read the story encouraging children to join in. (CL1)

## Physical Development
- Play 'Simon says', emphasising the names of body parts in the instructions. (PD1)
- Experiment with travelling and balancing using different body parts. (PD1)
- Play with balls and compare the way they move when they are thrown and kicked. Which parts of our bodies can we use to makethe ball move? (PD1)

## Personal, Social and Emotional Development
- Make a collection of objects familiar to the children which can be used in a foot feely box. Children should take it in turns to feel an object with their feet and describe it to the rest of the group. After the game has finished, talk about whether it is easier to use feet or hands for this activity and why. (PSE1)
- Use a large picture of a child as the focus for a discussion on body parts and how useful they are. For example, the nose can smell and act as a filter for dust and smoke particles. (PSE3)

## Literacy
- Help children to write name labels for a display of self-portraits. (L2)
- Involve the children in taking digital photographs of each other. Mount each photograph on a large sheet of card. Encourage the children to make pages for a body big book. Children could 'write' their birthdays, their eye colour, their shoe size, what they like to eat, what they like to do and any, interesting facts about their bodies. (L2)

## Mathematics
- Help children to draw round their feet. Compare feet sizes and use them as a non-standard measure for a variety of lengths. (M2)
- Use *Funnybones* by Janet and Allan Ahlberg as the stimulus for comparing sizes of dolls and teddies and to reinforce associated language for size. (M2)
- Play a game similar to Beetle Drive, in which children throw a dice and each number corresponds to a part of the body. (M1)

## Understanding the World
- Draw around a child. Label different parts of the body (see activity opposite). (UW2)
- Provide materials for children to make skeletons. They might like to stick white paper straws on black card, paint or chalk in white on black paper or lay plastic straws in the sand tray. (UW2)
- To reinforce names of body parts make jointed people from card pieces with brass fasteners for the joints. (UW2)

# Expressive Arts and Design

● Sing 'Heads, shoulders, knees and toes'. (EAD1)
● Paint self-portraits (see activity opposite). (EAD1)
● Explore which parts of the body can be used to make sounds to accompany songs. Children could clap, tap, click fingers, sniff, whistle, stamp, slap thighs, tap teeth, and so on. Encourage children to explore how the sounds can be made louder, quieter, faster and slower. (EAD2)

# Activity: Self-portraits

**Learning opportunity:** Painting based on close observation.

**Early Learning Goal:** Expressive Arts and Design. Exploring and using media and materials.

**Resources:** Ready-mixed paints in a range of colours so that children can pick the appropriate skin, hair and eye colours; plastic mirrors; photographs of people familiar to the group.

**Key vocabulary:** Names of colours, parts of the body, portrait.

**Organisation:** Small group.

**What to do:** Show children the photographs. Who are in the photos? What are the people wearing? What colours are their hair? Show children the paints. Pick one person in the photos. Ask the group which paint they would choose for that person's hair if they were to do a portrait. What would they use for the skin? Explain to the children that they are going to paint self-portraits. Talk about the need to choose colours carefully so that everyone will be able to recognise them from the pictures. As children paint, encourage them to notice where eyes should be positioned, and how arms and legs are placed in relationship to their bodies.

# Activity: Labelling body parts

**Learning opportunity:** Recognising and labelling parts of the body.

**Early Learning Goal:** Understanding the World. The world.

**Resources:** Large plain paper as long as a child; thick, black wax crayon; labels of the body parts.

**Key vocabulary:** Eye, ear, mouth, nose, head, arm, neck, elbow, hand, shoulder, tummy/stomach, waist, knee, foot, finger, toe (**Note:** The number and type of words to be used will vary from group to group.)

**Organisation:** Small group sitting on the floor.

**What to do:** Introduce the activity with a quick game of 'Point to your .....' in order to assess which body part names children are already familiar with.

Explain to the group that they are going to make a large poster to teach people the names for parts of the body. Show the children some of the labels. Can anyone recognise any of the words? What sounds do the words begin with?

Choose a child who is wearing shorts or trousers to lie down on the large piece of paper and draw round with the wax crayon. Ask the children to help you stick the labels on to the poster. Mount the poster at floor height.

# Display

Mount the body poster at floor height. As the weeks progress put out other labels for children to add to the body. Make a track of the feet used for measuring going to the body as if the body has walked all over the wall. Display the skeletons on a board near a table containing other books in the *Funnybones* series.

Cut around the portraits and mount on black sugar paper. Display the portraits against a background of a play area as if the children are enjoying a playtime together.

# Theme 2: Hands

## Communication and Language
- Clap children's names and encourage them to recognise their own and those of friends. (CL1)
- Prepare a feely bag of objects found in the classroom. Ask children to take it in turns to describe what they feel. (CL3)
- Talk about why and when people shake hands. Who has had their hand shaken? Discuss which hand is shaken and reinforce 'right' and 'left'. For a week encourage children to shake hands with you each day when they arrive or before going home. (CL2)

## Physical Development
- Encourage the development of fine motor skills by using construction toys with small pieces. (PD1)
- Play catching and throwing games. (PD1)
- Explore what hands can do to squeeze, roll and flatten playdough. (PD1)
- Outside use hands to enjoy 'painting' with water and large brushes. (PD1)
- Talk abour the importance of washing hands before eating and going to the toilet. Encourage children to become independent. (PD2)

## Personal, Social and Emotional Development
- Provide materials to make paper bag puppets. Encourage the children to choose their own resources and to use the puppets in their play. (PSE1)
- During circle time play games in which children pass on claps of differing numbers and rhythms. Encourage children to listen and to take turns. (PSE3)

## Literacy
- Draw around children's hands and help them to fill their hands with words for things they can do with their hands. Once full, cut them out. (L2)
- Use fingers to enjoy writing in trays of coloured sand. (L2)

## Mathematics
- Use a variety of finger rhymes to reinforce numbers one to five. (M1)
- Use ready mixed paint to make a hand print for each child. When dry, cut around the prints and compare the sizes. Use the prints as leaves and ask the children to stick them on a large painted tree. Encourage the use of positional language as the children talk about where their 'leaves' have been stuck. (M2)
- Outside measure lengths in hand spans. (M2)
- Play the handy estimation game (see activity opposite). (M1)

## Understanding the World
- Make thumb prints. Use magnifiers to explore the different patterns and see how they are all different (see activity opposite). (UW1)
- Compare hands. Help children to notice differences in palm lines, nail colours and sizes. Make a hand print in clay or dough. (UW1)
- In role-play use technology that requires fingers to push buttons (UW3)

## Expressive Arts and Design
- Use finger paints to make prints with fingers. Add lines and dots to turn the prints into small creatures. Encourage children to talk about their creatures. Where do they live? What can they do? What do they eat? (EAD1)
- Sing favourite songs and take it in turns to clap the rhythm. (EAD1)
- Provide a range of materials for children to choose from to make their own models. As they work,

encourage them to talk about what their hands are doing. (EAD1, 2)

● On black paper draw around a child's hand with white chalk several times so that the shapes touch and form a pattern. Ask children to choose three colours with which to paint their hand pattern. (EAD1)

# Activity: Handy estimation game

**Learning opportunity:** Estimating and counting numbers to ten.

**Early Learning Goal:** Mathematics. Numbers.

**Resources:** A basket of small objects (for example, Unifix cubes) such that a child's handful would be no more than ten; number cards for numerals to nine.

**Key vocabulary:** Numbers to ten, more, less than, fewer.

**Organisation:** Small group.

**What to do:** Invite a child to pick a handful of cubes from the basket. Ask the child to count how many there are. Ask another child to try and pick out a handful which has about the same number of cubes in it. How many are there? Is it the same number? Are there more/fewer cubes in the second handful? Continue this activity until all children have had a chance to be both the first picker and the second.

Next, show children a number card. Ask them to try to pick out quickly from the basket exactly the same number of cubes. Encourage children to do this by estimating rather than by counting. If appropriate, extend the game by asking children to pick up more/fewer cubes. On further occasions the language of addition/subtraction can also be used.

# Activity: Thumb prints

**Learning opportunity:** Observing and describing thumb prints.

**Early Learning Goal:** Understanding the World. People and communities.

**Resources:** Wide sticky tape; scissors; white chalk; magnifiers; postcard sized pieces of black sugar paper.

**Key vocabulary:** Thumb, print.

**Organisation:** Small group.

**What to do:** Explain to the children that thumbs can make prints and that everybody's print is different. Ask the group to look at their thumb prints with the magnifiers. What can they see? Hand out pieces of white chalk and show the children how to cover their thumb prints with chalk dust. Being careful not to finger the sticky part of the tape, cut a piece and hold it firmly at each end. Ask a child to place their thumb in the centre on the sticky side and lift it off. Stick the tape on a piece of black sugar paper and let the child examine it. Repeat the sticky tape exercise for each child's left and right thumb, remembering to name each one. Help children to notice the different patterns and to draw what they see on white paper.

**Note:** Although the above method produces clear prints, some groups may wish to use finger paint for a simpler way to make prints on paper.

# Display

With the children paint two large tree trunks with branches. Ask them where they want to stick their hand prints and handy words. Encourage them to explain the positions they choose rather than letting them simply point. On a nearby table place the clay hand prints and the thumb prints along with two magnifiers.

# Theme 3: Listening

## Communication and Language

- When sharing a story talk about the importance of being a good listener. Emphasise that in order to show we are listening to someone we need to look at them as they speak. (CL1)
- Go on a walk to detect sounds. Before the walk discuss what children will need to do. Use technology to record some of the sounds. After the walk discuss what the sounds were and how and why they were made. (CL2, 3)

## Physical Development

- Play games in which a whistle is blown or a drum is tapped a certain number of times to signify an action such as two taps means jump, one tap means hop and three taps means sit down. (PD1)
- Play 'The keeper of the keys' (see activity opposite). (PD1)
- Play musical statues, encouraging children to move in time with music. When the music stops ask the children to make a shape (e.g. be a tree) or perform an action (e.g. kneel tall) (PD1)

## Personal, Social and Emotional Development

- Enjoy using toy telephones and mobile phones for role-play. Encourage the children to initiaite the themes for their play and help them to find additonal resources to enhance the play (PSE3)
- Tell the traditional tale of *The boy who cried wolf*. Talk about the boy and why he should not have cried for help when he did not need it. (PSE2)
- Make a collection of precious objects which make a sound, such as a china bell, a baby's rattle and a bunch of keys. Explain to the children why each object is precious. Talk about the need to handle precious objects with care. Do the group think they can pass them around so carefully that they will not make a sound? (PSE3)

## Literacy

- Begin a word bank of words which rhyme with 'ear'. (L2)
- Read *Peace at Last* by Jill Murphy. Write a group version with new sounds (see activity opposite). (L2)
- Make a collection of books, familiar to the children. Encourage the children to enjoy reading to peers and also listening as friends share books. (L1)

## Mathematics

- Play number lotto and other games where children need to listen to instructions. (M1)
- Cut out a variety of different sizes and shapes of ears from card. Ask children to sort the ears according to shape and then to arrange each set in order of size. (M2)
- Provide each child with a small drum or shaker. Use these for counting activities. Ask children to shake/hit a given number of times. Ask them to count your taps/ hits and to copy. Can they do one more hit? (M1)

## Understanding the World

- Record each child saying 'good morning'. Play the recording to the children. Can they identify their own voice? How does it compare to their normal speaking voice? (UW2)
- Use a xylophone or glockenspiel to explore high and low notes. Invite children to design and make their own musical instruments and to describe the sounds they make. (UW2)
- Enjoy using CDs to explore music and well known songs. Talk about what is heard and also other technology that could be used instead of CDs (UW3)

## Expressive Arts and Design

- Ask children to listen to extracts of *Peter and the Wolf.* Encourage children to make up dances to the music. (EAD2)
- Use *Peace at Last* by Jill Murphy or a similar book to which children can add percussion for sound effects. Record the story and sounds. Later enjoy listening to the recording. (EAD1)
- Sing and make up actions for the song 'Do your ears hang low? in *Okki-tokki-unga: Action Songs for Children.* (EAD1)

## Activity: Peace at last

**Learning opportunity:** Collaborating to write and make a big book based on *Peace at Last.*

**Early Learning Goal:** Literacy. Writing.

**Resources:** *Peace at Last* (big book version if possible); large pieces of card or stiff paper for book pages; a variety of crayons, pencils and felt pens; a flip chart; a favourite doll or teddy owned by the group.

**Key vocabulary:** Vocabulary within *Peace at Last,* title, author, illustrator.

**Organisation:** Whole group introduction. Small groups for writing.

**What to do:** At the beginning of the week read *Peace at Last* to the group. To introduce the writing of a big book, ask children to help retell the *Peace at Last* story by using the pictures in the book. Draw attention to details in the pictures and encourage all children to join in repeating phrases such as 'I can't stand this!'

Talk to children about the noises they hear when they go to bed at night. Can they describe the sounds? Explain that together they are going to write a story about the group's doll/teddy who finds it difficult to get to sleep. Discuss who else might be in the story.

On the flip chart list the sounds that might be included in the story. Encourage children to think of their own ideas as well as those in the book by Jill Murphy. Over the week invite small groups to write a page for the group's book.

## Activity: The keeper of the keys

**Learning opportunity:** Moving quietly with control. Collaborating to play a circle game.

**Early Learning Goal:** Physical Development. Moving and handling.

**Resources:** Large bunch of keys.

**Key vocabulary:** Quietly, slowly, keys, blindfold, guard.

**Organisation:** Whole group.

**What to do:** After a warm-up activity which encourages children to listen, arrange them sitting on the floor in a large circle. Show everyone the keys. Ask the children to shut their eyes and listen to the sound the keys make as they are picked up. Ask if anyone thinks they could pick them up without making a sound. Allow two children to demonstrate.

Pick a child to be 'The keeper of the keys' and to sit on a chair placed in the middle of the circle. Explain that the keeper has to guard the keys. If they hear someone approaching the keys they should point to where the sound is coming from. If they point at the correct person they have saved the keys. If someone manages to take the keys back to their place without being pointed at, the keys are lost. The keeper may only point five times. Explain that when everyone is sitting silently you will pick someone to try and take the keys.

Talk about the need to sit very still and, when picked, to move very slowly and quietly. When everyone has understood the game, blindfold the keeper and play until all children have had the chance to be either the keeper or the taker. The game can be extended by having more than one taker at a time and by reducing the number of points allowed to three.

## Display

Display the instruments which children have made on a table. On another table put out a selection of instruments along with *Peace at Last,* the group's own big book and other well-known picture books. Encourage pairs of children to use the instruments to make sound effects for the stories.

# Theme 4: Looking

## Communication and Language
- Encourage children to take turns whilst playing 'I spy'. Clues could be colour, initial sound or position. (CL1)
- Play blindfold games. (CL2)
- Share books such as *Where's Wally?* by Martin Handford or *1001 Things to Spot on the Farm* by Gillian Doherty which encourage children to look closely at the pictures, use descriptive vocabulary and discuss with others as things are found or cannot be seen. (CL1)

## Physical Development
- Talk about the importance of looking when playing with balls and bats. Allow free play, encouraging children always to keep their eyes on the ball. (PD1)
- Play a variety of aiming games such as skittles or throwing bean bags or balls into hoops or buckets. (PD1)
- Play a game where a coloured card is used to signify an action such as jump, walk or hop. Encourage children to keep a close eye on the colour card and to change their action as soon as the cards have been changed. (PD1)

## Personal, Social and Emotional Development
- Play with jigsaw puzzles. Encourage children to look closely at details as the fit pieces together. (PSE3)
- Involve the children in setting up and using a role play opticians. As a group decide how many can play in the area at a time and, also, how the resources should be organised (see the activity opposite). (PSE2, 3)

## Literacy
- Encourage children to practise letter formation by making eye charts for the role-play area. (L2)
- Write a group poem which begins with the line 'Through the window we can see...'. Encourage children to think of descriptive alliterations such as a tall towering tree, a brown, breaking brick. (L2)

## Mathematics
- Count how many children have each eye colour. Display the results as a bar chart (see activity opposite) (M1)

- Provide each child with a book made from two pieces of A4 paper folded in half. On each page write a number from one to five. Give each child a number of magazines/catalogues which have people in them and ask the children to cut out faces and stick the given number on each page. Use the books for counting and for introducing the idea of doubles – if there are two faces on a page there will be four eyes or two pairs. (M1)
- Help children to make spectacles for a teddy bear out of pipe cleaners and to talk about the shapes used for the eye pieces. Can children make square eye pieces? What would triangular ones look like? (M2)

## Understanding the World
- Invite an adult who wears glasses to talk to the group about their glasses and what happens when they go to the optician. (UW1)
- Talk about eyes and what eyelashes and eyebrows are for. Encourage children to notice the variety in eye colours and that all eyes are different even though many people have blue, brown, grey and green eyes. (UW1)
- Enjoy playing with safe kaleidoscopes and periscopes. (UW2)

## Expressive Arts and Design

- When painting, encourage children to look closely at shapes and colours. (EAD1)
- Cut out pairs of spectacle frames from card and let children decorate them with sequins and other shiny and bright materials. Put them on sale in the optician role-play area. (EAD1)
- Enjoy trying on dressing up clothes and having fashion shows. Encourage children to do commentaries for what friends wear. (EAD2)

## Activity: Eye-colour bar chart

**Learning opportunity:** Collaborating to make a bar chart and comparing the number of children with different eye colours.

**Early Learning Goal:** Mathematics. Numbers.

**Resources:** Plastic mirrors; eyes cut from white paper; crayons in eye colours; a noticeboard with axes and labels for the bar chart at child height (see diagram); Blu-tack.

**Key vocabulary:** Bar chart, colours for eye colours, numbers sufficient to count the eyes, more, less.

**Organisation:** Whole group.

**What to do:** Whilst sitting in a circle on the floor talk about eye colours. Ask children in turn to say their eye colour. Where children are uncertain provide a mirror for them to check. Show the group the cut out eyes. Explain that they will be used to make a record of their eye colours. Invite children in turn to select a crayon the same colour as their eyes and to go and colour their iris. Once coloured, help children to stick their eye on the pre-prepared bar chart. As a group use the bar chart to count how many children have each eye colour. Which colour of eye do most children have? Do more children have blue or brown eyes?

## Activity: Optician role-play area

**Learning opportunity:** Playing collaboratively in a role play situation.

**Early Learning Goal:** Personal, Social and Emotional Development. Self-confidence and self-awareness. Managing feelings and behaviour.

**Resources:** A role-play area set out as an optician's with: a white coat/shirt; a telephone; a diary; a selection of toy spectacles; plastic sun glasses and home made glasses; a mirror; a letter chart; a till.

**Key vocabulary:** Spectacles, glasses, eye test.

**Organisation:** Whole group introduction with small groups using the area.

**What to do:** Involve children in the setting up of the optician's. Let them make eye testing charts and spectacles. Introduce the area to the whole group and talk about the items in it. Talk about the way an optician tests eyesight and the importance of helping customers to buy spectacles that they will be happy to wear. Together decide how many children the area can accommodate at a time and also how the area should be left at the end of play. Invite a small group to play in the optician's and over the coming days encourage all children to take on a variety of roles. Listen for suggestions of additional resources children would like included.

## Display

Mount and display the children's paintings as an art gallery. Number the pictures and make a catalogue of titles suggested by the children.

Around the bar chart place question cards which encourage children to extract information. Ask how many children have each eye colour? Which colour do most children have? Near the role-play area display the spectacles made by children with price labels and a mirror.

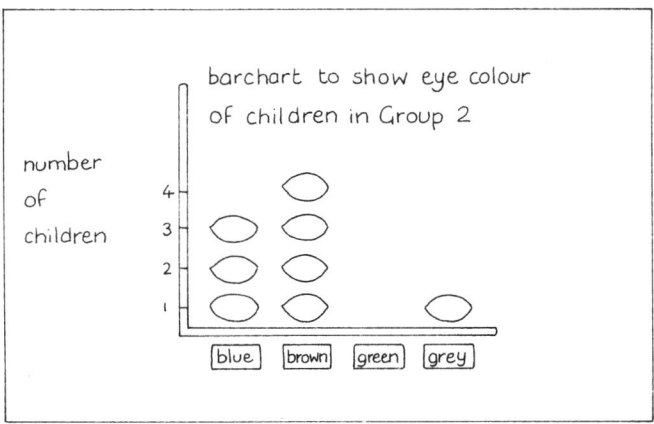

# Theme 5: Health

## Communication and Language

- Read a story which features food such as *Oliver's Fruit Salad* by Vivian French (Hodder Children's Books). Talk about favourite foods. (CL1)
- Talk about things people can do to be healthy such as eating fruit and vegetables, washing hands before eating and using hankies. Encourage children to talk about what they and their families do. (CL3)

## Physical Development

- Talk about the importance of gradually using different parts of our bodies in a warm-up before doing an activity which involves a lot of movement. Do a 'follow my leader' warm-up and talk about which parts of the body are being used (see activity opposite). (PD1)
- Set up a variety of challenges which involve both fine motor and gross motor skills. Examples include spooning water from one container to another, threading beads, stacking cubes, catching a ball, dribbling a ball, jumping, skipping. Repeat these activities a number of times over the week and show children how practice can help us to improve. (PD1)
- Talk about the kinds of foods which are good to eat. Provide each child with a sandwich box made from a piece of A4 card folded in half. Ask children to make healthy packed lunches either by cutting pictures out of magazines or by drawing. (PD2)

## Personal, Social and Emotional Development

- Talk about the kind of clothes that children wear when playing outside during different times of the year. Discuss how this can help to keep us healthy (see activity opposite). (PSE1)
- Invite parents who enjoy physical activities such as playing football or running marathons to talk to the children about what they do and how the activities help them to be healthy. Encourage children to try new activities outside. (PSE1)

## Literacy

- With the children make a healthy eating cafe. Encourage the children to make menus and to write orders. (L1, 2)
- Share a book that includes healthy food such as *Harda's Surprise* by Eileen Browne (Walker Books). Which foods in the story would the children like to eat? Ask children to retell the story using the pictures as a reminder of events. Also encourage them to read familiar words. (L1)

## Mathematics

- Provide each child with basket and a list of healthy foods for them to place in their basket (for example: 4 apples, 2 carrots, 3 bottles of water). The foods could be toy foods, real ones or pictures. (M1)
- Repeat the basket activity but this time provide the foods and ask the children to make the shopping list. (M1)
- Buy and sell food in the role play cafe. (M1)
- Enjoy following a recipe for a healthy food (for example fruit salad, fruit smoothie). (M2)

## Understanding the World

- Having first checked for children's food allergies, try taste testing for a variety of fruits and raw vegetables. (UW2)
- Talk about places in the local environment where children enjoy playing and ones which are disliked. Talk about safety, why the places are liked or disliked and how children might like to change them. (UW2)

## Expressive Arts and Design

- Use pastels or chalks to make pictures of fruit and vegetables. (EAD1)
- On paper plates use tissue paper or playdough to make a healthy meal. (EAD2)
- Weave place mats for the healthy cafe. (EAD1)
- Print with vegetables and hard fruits. (EAD1)

## Activity: Warming Up

**Learning opportunity:** Moving with control and following instructions.

**Early Learning Goal:** Physical Development. Moving and handling.

**Resources:** Large space.

**Key vocabulary:** Circle, fast, slow, quietly, parts of the body.

**Organisation:** Whole group.

**What to do:** Sitting on the floor, talk to children about the importance of gradually warming up before they begin very active activities and games. Hold up a hand and ask children which parts can move. Do a variety of finger and wrist exercises and ask children to copy. Gradually continue with other parts of the body, encouraging children to recognise which parts are being exercised. Once all parts have been warmed up, play a favourite whole group game which involves running. Finally, cool down by playing sleeping lions where children lie on the ground as if asleep.

## Activity: Wearing the right clothes

**Learning opportunity:** Picking and wearing clothes to suit a variety of weather conditions and temperatures.

**Early Learning Goal:** Personal, Social and Emotional Development. Self-confidence and self-awareness.

**Resources:** A large box containing a variety of items of clothing including ones for cold, wet and sunny weather such as a scarf, wellington boots, a sun hat and a raincoat; pictures of people dressed sensibly for a variety of weathers.

**Key vocabulary:** Names of clothing in the basket, wet, hot, cold, sunny, rainy, summer, winter.

**Organisation:** Whole group.

**What to do:** Show the pictures of the people. Ask children what the people are wearing and why the items of clothing would be sensible ones to wear. Show the group the clothes that are in the basket. Ask a child to come and pick something which would be good to wear on a sunny day and to put it on. Ask why it would be good. What else would be useful on a sunny day? Think about the sunscreen, sunglasses and clothes with sleeves. Repeat the activity for a variety of weathers and times of year. Encourage children to dress independently and to think of safety issues as well as the weather. For example, it would not be sensible to wear mittens if playing on a climbing frame. Encourage the children to enjoy using the clothes for role-play.

## Display

On a large board put up a paper tablecloth and make a picnic display with the paper plates of healthy foods. Display the playdough foods on a table in front.

On a second board, stick up the pictures showing people in a variety of clothing and place the basket of clothes nearby. Invite children to enjoy wearing them as they visit the healthy cafe and for their own choice of role-play situations.

# Theme 6: Faces

←string

## Communication and Language
- Together plan a 'Disguises Day'. Talk about the activities children would like to happen and the jobs that will have to be done for the day to take place. (CL3)
- As a group look for faces within picture books. Encourage children to consider why the faces are happy, sad, worried...(CL2)

## Physical Development
- Tell the story of a spy putting on his disguise and encourage children to mime to the story. (PD1)
- Play shadow games in which children are the spies who are trying to track you. Stress the importance of only moving when you move and trying to keep in your shadow. (PD1)
- Draw with chalk on the playground a variety of large faces with flowing hair. Use them for aiming games and for walking on the lines. (PD1)

## Personal, Social and Emotional Development
- In circle time, talk about the importance of smiling. At the end of the session pass a smile around the circle (see activity opposite). (PSE2)
- Declare a 'Smile Week' in which children will try to make people feel happy by smiling at them. (PSE3)

## Literacy
- Provide magazines from which children can cut faces. Encourage them to stick faces in small books and write captions such as happy, sad and cross. (L2)
- Make 'smile please' posters. (L2)
- In small groups complete sentences such as, 'I am sad when...' or 'I am happy when...'. Enjoy reading the written sentences. (L1, 2)

## Mathematics
- Use the face as the stimulus for counting activities with a small group. Count how many ears, eyes, noses and mouths the group has. Encourage them to notice that the number of eyes is the same as the number of ears. As children begin to notice similarities, ask them to predict how many chins the group will have. (M1)
- Provide children with drawings of half faces. Encourage children to complete the pictures to make symmetrical faces. Use plastic mirrors to check the faces are symmetrical. (M2)
- Provide each child with a selection of sticky paper regular shapes. Ask them to make pictures of faces. Encourage the children to talk about the shapes they use for the eyes, nose, mouth and ears. (M2)

## Understanding the World
- Use mirrors or digital photographs to allow children to observe their own faces and then make paper-plate face masks. (UW1)
- Give descriptions of children to the group and ask them to say who you are describing. As you play, help children to realise the differences and similarities they have with peers. (UW1)
- Share photos of events children celebrate. Look at faces and talk about the emotions they show. Did children enjoy the events? Why/why not? (UW1)

## Expressive Arts and Design
- Make happy face mobiles by cutting card faces, decorating both sides and stringing them together (see diagram above). (EAD1)
- Sing 'If you're happy and you know it clap your hands' (Traditional). Encourage children to suggest emotions and actions e.g.
  *If you're angry and you know it shake your head.*
  *If you're sad and you know it have a hug.* (EAD1)
- Make two-faced puppets which smile and cry from paper plates (see activity opposite). (EAD2)
- Use pasta, string and wool to make collages of faces. These are particularly effective if they are sprayed with silver or gold paint when dry. (EAD2)

# Activity: Smiling

**Learning opportunity:** Working collaboratively, listening to others and talking with feeling.

**Early Learning Goal:** Personal, Social and Emotional Development. Managing feelings and behaviour.

**Resources:** A hand puppet.

**Key vocabulary:** Smile, happy.

**Organisation:** Whole group sitting on the floor in a circle.

**What to do:** Remind the group of the routines for circle time and the importance of always looking at the person who is speaking. Praise those who are already looking at you as you talk.

Show the group your puppet. Tell the group its name and that it is very special to you because whenever you see it you smile. Ask the children how they feel when someone smiles at them. What makes them smile?

Pass the puppet around the circle. Whoever holds the puppet has the opportunity to speak. Once all the children who want to have spoken, talk about the importance of smiles for helping us to feel good. Finish by 'passing a smile' around the circle.

# Activity: Happy/Sad puppets

**Learning opportunity:** Using a variety of materials to make puppets and using the puppets in imaginative, and role play situations.

**Early Learning Goal:** Expressive Arts and Design. Being imaginative.

**Resources:** Selection of scraps of material, paper, wool, sequins; felt pens; ready mixed paints; glue; scissors; an example of a paper-plate puppet clown. For each child: two small paper plates, card to make the hat and a thick 30cm long piece of dowelling or cardboard tubing.

**Key vocabulary:** Names of materials and colours being used, happy, sad.

**Organisation:** Small group.

**What to do:** Show the group the example of the puppet. Show them that it has two faces and ask why that would be useful in a play. Let the group ask the clown some questions.

Give each child a plate and ask them to draw a happy face on the underneath/non waxy side. Remind children of where they need to position the eyes. Repeat this with the sad face. Finally, stick strips of paper or wool on for hair. When dry, stick the plates together with glue with the dowelling/card tube stuck inside for the neck/handle. (See diagram.)

Make hats from card and glue them on to the heads. When completely dry, the children can use their puppets to make up plays, tell stories, take on safe walks or simply be friends that listen and talk.

# Display

Display the face collages with a 'smile please!' poster on a board and hang the smiling mobiles close by. Cover a table with a cloth and carefully place the clown puppets on it. To the side arrange a table or large box as a puppet theatre for children to use their puppets in. Also include a book of tickets and till so that children can sell tickets for their shows.

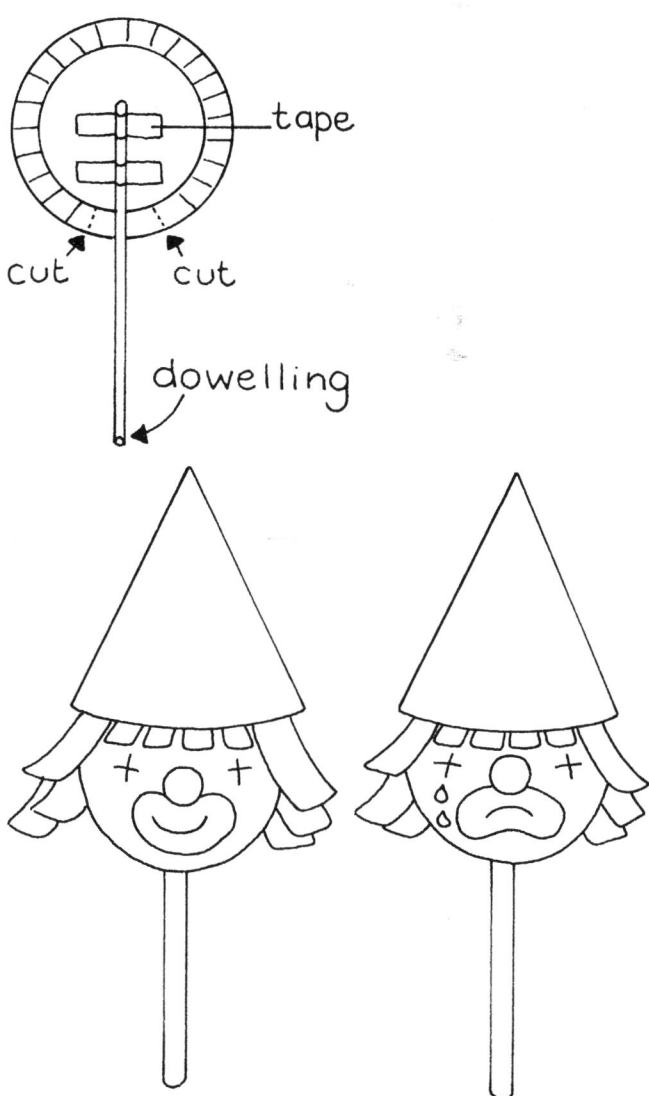

# Bringing it all together

## A day of disguises

Explain to the children that they are going to have 'a day of disguises'. They will learn how to disguise themselves. At the end there will be a special disguise parade to which parents and friends will be invited to come.

The event will work best if it is held in a large room/hall where a variety of activities can be set out for children to visit in turn. Divide the children into small groups of about four children with an adult. Give each child a piece of card which is set out as a passport to be completed during the event. Allocate each group to an activity and explain the direction in which they will move. Make sure that the adults have ideas for games such as 'I spy', which they could play with their group should an activity finish before it is time to move on. If enough adults are available it is useful to have each activity run by a different person whilst others move round with the children.

## Activities

- Having first checked that children are not allergic to face paints, invite adults to come in and help give children a new look.
- Put out passport photograph sized pieces of paper and crayons for children to record their new face and stick it in the passport.
- Talk to children about the way people can often be recognised from a long way off by how they move. Challenge the children to try walking in a variety of ways as if they were someone else. Help them to practise the walk they will use in the disguise parade.
- Talk to children about their names and their ages. For their disguise they will need a new name and age. Help children to record these in their passports.
- Make a collection of clothes which children can dress up in for their disguise. Collect enough for children to be able to keep the clothes on for the whole event.
- Use an ink pad to record children's thumb and finger prints.
- Talk about clothes and the way we often recognise people from the things they wear. Make a collection of shoes owned by children in the group. Play a game in which children have to recognise their own shoes and then identify those of friends. Before playing, check that all shoes are named but cover the names up for the game.
- Give each child a sheet containing nine outlines of identical faces. Invite the children to add lines to disguise the faces.

- Invite a parent with a digital camera to take photos of the complete disguise for the passports.

## Food

Although food is not a requirement for a 'disguises event' most children and adults will enjoy some refreshments after the parade.

**Involve the children in preparing food:**

- Make face biscuits by using melted chocolate, icing tubes and sweets to decorate plain biscuits.
- Make a 'disguised cocktail' by mixing a selection of fruit juices and adding small pieces of cut-up soft fruits. Can children identify which fruits and juices are in the cocktail?

## The parade

After all the disguise activities have been done, ask children to sit on the floor in a circle. Arrange chairs around the circle for parents and friends. Put on some quiet, background music to which children will enjoy parading, such as the theme music to the *Pink Panther*. Invite children in turn to tell everyone their new name and age, and to walk around the circle in role. Once all those who want to parade have done so, share the biscuits and fruit cocktail.

Planning
for Learning
through
**All about me**

# Resources

## Resources to collect

- Pictures of faces from magazines
- Sequins
- Plastic mirrors
- Kaleidoscopes
- Periscopes
- Clothes for making disguises.

## Everyday resources:

- Boxes e.g. cereal packets, shoe boxes
- Variety of papers and cards such as sugar, tissue, silver and shiny papers, wallpaper and corrugated card
- Paint, different sized paint brushes and a variety of paint mixing containers
- A variety of pencils, crayons, pastels and felt pens
- Glue and scissors
- Decorative and finishing materials such as sequins, foils, glitter, tinsel, shiny wool and threads, beads, pieces of textiles and parcel ribbon
- Table covers
- Malleable materials such as play-dough
- Paper plates
- Dowel
- Pasta.

## Stories

- *Funnybones* by Janet and Allan Ahlberg
- *Handa's Surprise* by Eileen Browne
- *The Shopping Basket* by John Burningham
- *Oliver's Fruit Salad* by Vivian French
- *Oliver's Vegetables* by Vivian French
- *Where's Wally?* by Martin Handford
- *Peace at Last* by Jill Murphy
- *Lulu's Lunch* by Camilla Reid.

## Non-Fiction

- *1001 Things to Spot on Holiday* by Hazel Maskell
- *1001 Things to Spot in Town* by Anna Milbourne
- *The Usborne Flip-Flap Body Book* by Alastair Smith and Judy Tatchell.

## Songs

- *Okki-tokki-unga: Action Songs for Children* chosen by Beatrice Harrop, Linda Friend and David Gadsby.

## Poems

- *Out and About* by Shirley Hughes
- *This little Puffin* by Elizabeth Matterson
- *Mustard, Custard, Grumble Belly and Gravy* by Michael Rosen and Quentin Blake.

## Resources for planning

- **England:** Department for Education 'Statutory Framework for the Early Years Foundation Stage' (http://www.foundationyears.org.uk/eyfs-statutory-framework/)
- **Northern Ireland:** CCEA 'Northern Ireland Curriculum' (www.nicurriculum.org.uk/foundation_stage/)
- **Scotland:** Learning and Teaching Scotland: 'Pre-birth to Three: Positive Outcomes for Scotland's Children and Families' (www.ltscotland.org.uk/earlyyears/)
- **Wales:** Welsh Government: 'Framework for children's learning for 3 to 7 year olds in Wales' (http://wales.gov.uk/topics/educationandskills/earlyyearshome/foundation-phase/?lang=en).

# Collecting evidence of children's learning

Monitoring children's development is an important task. Making a profile of children's achievements, strengths, capabilities interests and learning will help you to see progress and will draw attention to those who are having difficulties for some reason. If a child needs additional professional help, such as speech therapy, these cumulative profiles will provide valuable evidence.

Profiles should cover all the areas of learning, as defined by the relevant UK framework, and be the result of collaboration between practitioners, parents and carers. Parents should be made aware of your record keeping policies when their child joins your group. Show parents the types of documentation that you are keeping and make sure they understand their purpose. As a general rule, documentation should be open. Families should have access to their child's documentation at any time and know they can contribute to it. Take regular opportunities to talk to parents about children's progress. If you have formal discussions regarding children about whom you have particular concerns, a dated record of the main points should be kept.

## Keeping it manageable

Documentation should be helpful in informing practitioners, adult helpers and parents and always be for the benefit of the child. The golden rule is to keep it simple, manageable and useful. Do not try to make records following every activity!

Documentation will basically fall into two categories – observations and reflections:

## Observations

- **Spontaneous observations:** Sometimes you will want to make a note of observations as they happen e.g. a child is heard counting cars accurately during a play activity, or is seen to play collaboratively for the first time.

- **Planned observations:** Sometimes you will plan to make observations of children's developing skills within a planned activity. Using the learning opportunity identified for an activity will help you to make appropriate judgments about children's capabilities, strengths and interests, and to record them systematically.

**To collect information:**

- Talk to children about their activities and listen to their responses.
- Listen to children talking to each other.
- Observe children's work such as early writing, drawings, paintings and models. (Keeping photocopies or photographs can be useful in tracking progress. Photographs are particularly useful to monitor children's development in the outdoor environment.)

Sometimes it may be appropriate to set up 'one off' activities for the purposes of monitoring development. Some groups at the beginning of each term, for example, ask children to write their name and to make a drawing of themselves to record their progressing skills in both co-ordination and observation.

## Reflections

It is useful to spend regular time reflecting on the children's progress. Aim to make some comments about each child each week, and discuss these regularly with colleagues and families.

## Informing your planning

Collecting evidence about children's progress is time consuming and it is important that it is useful. When planning, use the information collected to help you to decide what learning opportunities you need to provide next for each child. For example, a child who has poor pencil or brush control will benefit from more play with dough or construction toys to build strength of muscles in the hands and fingers.

## Example observation sheet

**Name:** Lucy Field

**Date:** 17.1.15

**Area of Learning:** Mathematics. Count reliably with numbers from 1 to 20.

**Context (Please tick):**

**Child-initiated:** √    **Adult-led:**

**Alone:**    **In a group:** √

**Observation:** Lucy is playing outside with two friends. She is trying to build the tallest tower and counting the bricks. "1, 2, 3, 4, 5, 7, 8. Mine's 8. Yours is only 7." She knocks the tower down, chuckles and starts to build again, counting as she places the bricks. "1, 2, 3, 4, 5, 7." The tower falls over. "Oh blow. I wanted to do 20."

**What next:** Check Lucy knows 6 follows 5. Encourage use of the outdoor counting grids, skittles and number rhyme CD.

**Observer:** E. M. Hogg

# Overview of areas covered through 'All about me'

| | Communication and Language | Physical Development | Personal, Social and Emotional Development | Literacy | Mathematics | Understanding the World | Expressive Arts and Design |
|---|---|---|---|---|---|---|---|
| My body | Listening and attention<br>Understanding<br>Speaking | Moving and handling<br>Health and self-care | Self-confidence and self-awareness<br>Managing feelings and behaviour<br>Making relationships | Reading<br>Writing | Numbers<br>Shape, space and measures | People and communities<br>The world<br>Technology | Exploring and using media and materials<br>Being imaginative |
| Hands | Listening and attention<br>Understanding<br>Speaking | Moving and handling<br>Health and self-care | Self-confidence and self-awareness<br>Managing feelings and behaviour<br>Making relationships | Reading<br>Writing | Numbers<br>Shape, space and measures | People and communities<br>The world<br>Technology | Exploring and using media and materials<br>Being imaginative |
| Listen-ing | Listening and attention<br>Understanding<br>Speaking | Moving and handling<br>Health and self-care | Self-confidence and self-awareness<br>Managing feelings and behaviour<br>Making relationships | Reading<br>Writing | Numbers<br>Shape, space and measures | People and communities<br>The world<br>Technology | Exploring and using media and materials<br>Being imaginative |
| Looking | Listening and attention<br>Understanding<br>Speaking | Moving and handling<br>Health and self-care | Self-confidence and self-awareness<br>Managing feelings and behaviour<br>Making relationships | Reading<br>Writing | Numbers<br>Shape, space and measures | People and communities<br>The world<br>Technology | Exploring and using media and materials<br>Being imaginative |
| Health | Listening and attention<br>Understanding<br>Speaking | Moving and handling<br>Health and self-care | Self-confidence and self-awareness<br>Managing feelings and behaviour<br>Making relationships | Reading<br>Writing | Numbers<br>Shape, space and measures | People and communities<br>The world<br>Technology | Exploring and using media and materials<br>Being imaginative |
| Faces | Listening and attention<br>Understanding<br>Speaking | Moving and handling<br>Health and self-care | Self-confidence and self-awareness<br>Managing feelings and behaviour<br>Making relationships | Reading<br>Writing | Numbers<br>Shape, space and measures | People and communities<br>The world<br>Technology | Exploring and using media and materials<br>Being imaginative |

Note: For each theme, highlight the Early Learning Goal areas covered through both adult focused and child-initiated activities relating to 'All about me'.

# Home links

The theme of All about me lends itself to useful links with children's homes and families. Through working together children and adults gain respect for each other and build comfortable and confident relationships.

## Establishing partnerships

- Keep parents informed about the activities for All about me. By understanding the activity of the group, parents will enjoy the involvement of contributing ideas, time and resources.
- Photocopy the family page for each child to take home.
- Invite friends, childminders and families to share all or part of the 'Day of disguises'.

## Visiting enthusiasts

- Invite adults to come in to talk about wearing spectacles and contact lenses.
- Invite adults who enjoy face painting to run an activity at the disguises event.

## Resource requests

- Ask parents to contribute clothes which are no longer needed for making disguises.
- Parcel bows, wrapping papers, wall papers and any interesting boxes and packaging are invaluable for collage work and a wide range of interesting activities.

## The day of disguises

- It is always useful to have extra adults at times such as the disguises event.
- Put out a suggestion box in which parents can contribute ideas for activities which could be used on the day of disguises.
- Invite parents to donate games such as 'Misfits' which fit with the disguises theme.